This book belongs to:

Draw a picture of yourself/self-portrait in the frame below

http://www.fast-print.net/bookshop

A catalogue record for this book is available from the British Library

ISBN 978-178456-415-5
(Also available as an e-book: ePub 978-178456-976-1 & Mobi/Kindle 978-178456-977-8)

First published 2016 by Fast-Print Publishing, Peterborough, England.

Music is Medicine

For Hazel, Tom, Luke & Zachary
for their love, support and understanding

"Music can minister to minds diseased,
pluck from the memory a rooted sorrow,
raze out the written troubles of the brain,
and with its sweet oblivious antidote,
cleanse the full bosom of all perilous stuff that
weighs upon the heart"

William Shakespeare

Contents

Acknowledgements

This book would not have been possible without the involvement of two remarkable women **Kate Williams** and **Farai Pfende**. Together we make up the Joco Team. They have worked tirelessly with me to develop the ideas, resources and courses that make up our **'Music in Care'** programme. Their belief in what we do, their passion, professionalism, creativity and ability to take my muddled ramblings and turn them into beautiful images and meaningful text is truly awesome.

Jeni Jones and the team at **Pancreatic Cancer UK** *(Charity No. 1112708)*

Robert Cornes and **Orchid Male Cancer Charity** *(Charity No. 1080540)*

Wayne Earle and my "Brothers in Arms"

Foreword

In early 2016 I found myself in the surreal world of being diagnosed with cancer. It is not somewhere you ever want or expect to be despite the high statistical probability. I found myself propelled into a new reality of uncertainty and vulnerability. The urgency and severity of the medical procedures was immediate with the understandable emphasis on the medical and highly technical procedures. This is neither surprising nor is it any way a complaint, I regard myself as very lucky to have received excellent treatment in such a timely, caring and professional manner.

One factor that added to the unreal nature of my position was that I was diagnosed with a cancer I, and many others, had never heard of, penile cancer. A condition so rare that only 500 men receive a diagnosis in the UK ever year. Like many other men with this condition I was being treated for something completely different for several months before happening to see someone who recognised the condition for what it truly was. Referrals were made to the specialist team in Leicester, one of the super-hubs across the country created to deal with this rare condition.

Under the care of **Jonathan Goddard, Consultant Urological Surgeon** and his remarkable team, I underwent three operations to remove the cancer and to ascertain if it had travelled anywhere else in my body. Treatment is undertaken in stages, with results taken at each stage, which dictate what needs to happen next. As a patient you are carried along on a tide of uncertainty and discomfort and one of the most difficult elements to cope with is the lack of ability to plan anything; you have to wait for the effects of one procedure to subside whilst waiting for the decision as to what to do next.

Initially, I found it difficult to cope with the psychological impact of my condition, or to find any information about it, and so I sought the fellowship of the men who had been through what I was experiencing. I found that connection from two sources to whom I will be eternally grateful. The first was **Robert Cornes**, Male Cancer Information Nurse Specialist with the **Orchid Male Cancer Charity**. Rob listened to my concerns and anxiety, providing invaluable practical advise and support. He also put me in touch with a remarkable group of men who are part of a Facebook group for **Penile Cancer Awareness and Support**. The courage and honesty of these remarkable men is inspirational and humbling. They have provided psychological support and understanding in a way that I could never have imagined possible via a social media platform, linking men across the world dealing with this often dreadful condition.

Like everyone undergoing serious medical interventions you find yourself in a position where you are being "done to" – you have little or no control over the processes that have to occur if you are to survive; a position which leaves you feeling powerless and impotent.

As a musician I have music with me all the time and I took music with me to appointments and to hospital treatment, playing those tracks that are the **'Soundtrack to My Life'** to help with the anxiety and the waiting. Music can transport us to another place, calm and soothe us. It allowed me to take particular people with me who live within the various tracks I had chosen.

My diagnosis occurred around the point of my first meeting with **Jeni Jones**, Nurse Specialist with **Pancreatic Cancer UK.** Farai and I were at a "Spirituality at End of Life" conference at **LOROS Hospice** in Leicester where we were running a workshop on **'My Story in Music'** - a project that we have developed for working with personalised music supporting those at end of life.

Jeni invited us to present at a "Living Well" day for people with pancreatic cancer and so in July 2016 we met a remarkable group of people dealing with this devastating condition. At first it was difficult to see what impression, if any, we were making. It was only during conversations over lunch that we realised that people were struggling to find the words to cope with their personal situation and the emotions that it brought; it was almost too risky to speak out in front of group members. People talked to us about the way they used music, not in a formal way but as a way to engage with emotions, channel feelings and express their fears. No one had thought of music as being something they could actively use during treatment to help cope with the experience and manage their anxieties. What follows is a way of using music to do just that and to take some control over what's happening to you.

Music is Medicine Core Principles

These are the values that underpin **'Music is Medicine'**. I ask you to bear them in mind as you complete this book.

When undergoing treatment it is important to:

- See the whole person not just the diagnosis

- Be open to the proven health benefits of music to aid healing and recovery

- Look beyond the required procedures and identify and nourish your psychological wellbeing.

Why Music?

Music is strongly linked to life events and experiences that define who we are. Music can transport us to a particular time or place and release strong emotions. It can calm and soothe us or motivate us and help us to find energy and drive. Music can greatly improve the quality of our lives.

Whilst undergoing medical treatment, music can:

- Impact your mood
- Aid relaxation
- Aid recovery and healing
- Tap into the energy you will need for the challenges to come
- Be a way of getting in touch with and helping to manage your thoughts, feelings and emotions
- Be a way of coping with a diagnosis and undergoing medical treatment

Music can provoke an emotional response even if you have never heard it before. However, if you choose to listen to music which is significant to you personally you will experience the benefits listed above in abundance. This is why 'Music is Medicine' was created.

In recognition of the amazing work they do and the impact they have had on me whilst writing this book, a proportion of the profits made will be shared with **Orchid Male Cancer Charity** and **Pancreatic Cancer UK**.

Using the Book

The book has been designed in such a way that it can be carried around with you and used whenever you will find it helpful. Having it with you when you attend appointments, treatments or admission to hospital can provide a much needed distraction to the medical necessities you are undergoing. The book, together with the music choices you make, will make for a better experience to help you to remain positive and assist your recovery.

REMEMBER!

- Take your time - enjoy!
- Don't be over-influenced by what other people think - this is YOUR **'Music is Medicine'**

- Involve people close to you to help recall memories and events if you wish

- There are no right or wrong answers! Please use the questions in the book as you choose. For example, if a question isn't relevant to you, leave it blank or if you have three favourite singers rather than one, record all three.

Recording

The questions within the **'Music is Medicine'** are designed to prompt you to think about people, events and feelings that may be important to you. Some questions may not be relevant to you and you may wish to leave them blank or change the question to something that works better for you.

In the space provided under each question, record the piece(s) of music including the artist(s) if that is significant. For example you may like 'Yesterday' by the Beatles but prefer a version recorded by Frank Sinatra.

It is important that you record the story of why that piece of music is important to you and the memories linked to it. Was it playing when you met your partner? Did you sing it with your family? Was it something you sang at church or school as a child? Each section also has a space to record your three **'Favourites'** from the category that will then transfer to you **'Playlist'** page.

Dislikes

You will find there is a section entitled **'Dislikes'** for you to record the music and sounds that you really don't want to hear. There is obviously no **'Favourites'** section on this page and you do not need to include anything from this section on your **'Playlist'** page.

Activities

Throughout the book, spaces have been left for you to record your thoughts, feelings, frustrations, hopes and fears. There are activities that you can undertake if you wish. For example, there are drawings that can be coloured in or left blank, spaces where sketches or pictures can be inserted. Just find your creativity as encouraged by the music choices you have made.

Journal pages have been included for you to record specific and important memories, thoughts and reflections that will help you to cope with the processes and procedures you are undertaking.

Did You Know?

We are hardwired for music!

The human body is actually rhythmic including our breathing, heartbeats and brain waves. We are also designed to distinguish music from the noises we hear and naturally respond to tunes, tones, beats, repetitions and rhythms.

To understand the impact of music it is important to get back to a time before the written word. The oral messages that were created were constructed in a way that ensured that the message was preserved, preventing people from making up their own messages. It helped to transfer culture and knowledge intact.

The construction of this early music incorporated patterns of sound which included alliteration, assonance, repetition and rhyme. These helped to predict what would happen next in the pattern of sounds.

"One thing about music when it hits you, you feel no pain."

Bob Marley

CALM REFLECTION - KEEPING ME GROUNDED

Music to relax to

Music to listen to alone

Music to share with others

Music that reminds me of who I am

Fill the thought bubble with pictures, words, drawings and memories of how to help you relax.

Music that can distract me from difficult thoughts

Music that helps me to sleep

Music that helps relieve my pain

Natural sounds I like to hear

JOURNAL: Use this page to record things that have helped you to remain calm and relaxed

My three favourites from CALM REFLECTION are:

1.

2.

3.

Add these to your playlist on Page 52

STAYING POSITIVE - KEEP FIGHTING

Music that gets me out of bed

Music I like to dance to

Music that channels my anger

Music that reassures me

Music that comes from my best time/era

Music that brings me out fighting

"MY HEART, WHICH IS SO FULL TO OVERFLOWING, HAS OFTEN BEEN SOLACED AND REFRESHED BY MUSIC WHEN SICK AND WEARY."

Martin Luther

Music that reminds me of good times

Music I enjoy singing along to

Music to celebrate to

Music anthems that motivate me

What would be the theme tune to a movie of your life?

JOURNAL: Use this page to record things that have helped you to remain positive

My three favourites from STAYING POSITIVE are:

1.

2.

3.

Add these to your playlist on Page 52

"The magic of
'musical medicine'
will come into its own.
The application of such
healing potencies will
not be limited just to man's
body and mind.
It will be an agency
for building and healing
his soul as well"

Corine Heline

FEELINGS - EMOTIONS

Music that makes me cry

Music that changes my mood

Fill the thought bubble with pictures, words, drawings and memories of the people, places, things that are the loves of your life.

Music that makes me sad

Music that makes me happy

Music that frightens me or makes me uneasy

Musical guilty pleasures

Music that makes me laugh or smile

Music to fall in love to or make love to

JOURNAL: Use this page to record your feelings and emotions and ways you found to cope with them.

My three favourites from FEELINGS are:

1.

2.

3.

Add these to your playlist on Page 52

SPIRITUALITY

Spirituality does not necessarily mean religion but is about what relates to or effects the human spirit or soul as opposed to material or physical things.

Favourite piece of spiritual or religious music

Music of my culture

What music will you hear in HEAVEN?
What music will you hear in HELL?

Music to get lost in

Music that brings me peace

Music that lifts my soul

Music to meditate to

"A wise man seeks by music to strengthen his soul, the thoughtless one uses it to stifle his fears"

Confucius

When does silence help?

Did you know?

Apollo was the Greek God of Music and Medicine

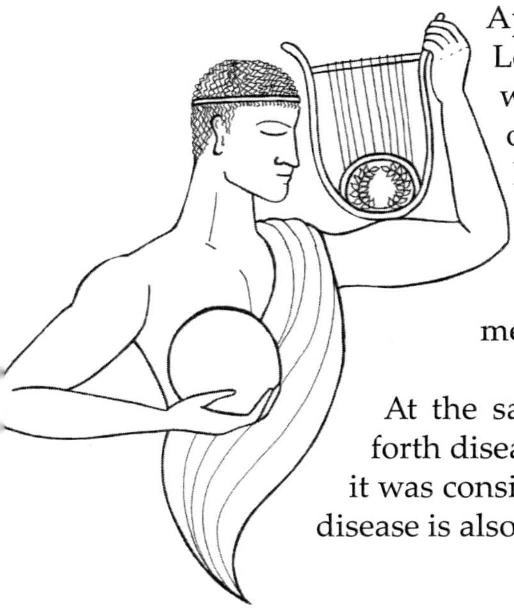

Apollo was the son of Zeus and Leto, twin brother of Artemis. He was the god of music, and is often depicted playing a golden lyre.

He was also known as the god of healing, giving the science of medicine to man.

At the same time, he could also bring forth disease and plague with his arrows; it was considered that a god that can cause disease is also able to prevent it.

JOURNAL: Use this page to record music that connects you to yourself or to something greater than yourself

My three favourites from SPIRITUALITY are:

1.

2.

3.

Add these to your playlist on Page 52

DISLIKES

Music genres I dislike

Particular artists I dislike

Particular songs or pieces I dislike

Particular songs or pieces that I find upsetting

Sounds that I dislike

Sounds that upset me

What music has you running for the 'OFF' switch?

JOURNAL: Use this page to record all of the other things that people need to know you want to avoid.

"Music is therapy. Music moves people. It connects people in ways that no other medium can. It pulls heart strings. It acts as medicine."

Macklemore

MY MUSIC IS MEDICINE PLAYLIST

Record your favourite songs from each section here in your playlist

1.

2.

3.

4.

5.

6.

7.

8.

9.

10.

11.

12.

Practical Application of 'Music is Medicine'

Once the book has been completed and the tracks of greatest significance have been chosen, it is possible to apply the music in practical and therapeutic ways. For this to be most effective it is important to record the reason why a particular song has been chosen on the memories page.

For example, if you know that a visit to the hospital can be upsetting, identify the songs from the toolkit that have the most relaxing and soothing impact and play these during the visit. Hearing these familiar and comforting songs will help to lessen the anxiety and divert you away from the distressing and anxious thoughts.

Similarly, if you find yourself disorientated and unsure of where you are, try using those songs that have been chosen to reconnect with familiar and reassuring aspects of the past e.g. those related to occupation, family or events. Hearing these songs can reconnect you to those people and places that give comfort and reassurance.

Creating the **'Music is Medicine'** can be of therapeutic value to family and friends who find visits emotionally difficult. Supporting you to collect music and recording it in your toolkit or helping you to access your music, is a useful way to spend a visit.

Technology

Your **'Music is Medicine'** toolkit enables you to have a comprehensive playlist of significant music for yourself or an individual. Accessing that music is the most important part of the process.

Music is becoming cheaper and more accessible using technology. There are several ways to use technology to listen to the music directly allowing you to listen wherever and whenever you wish.

Examples of places to access music online include:

- YouTube
- Spotify
- iTunes
- Apple Music
- Amazon Music

Existing Collections

You may already have CDs, records or cassettes that include your significant music and will enable you to access your music.

It is important that you have the right equipment to be able play your music. Using your existing player could be the easiest option as you may already have a full understanding of how to use it. Whatever is the easiest option for you is best but you may want to consider whether that option is portable should you wish to use music outside of your home. You may want to create a CD or MP3 collection of your **'Music is Medicine'** that you can use with a portable device and headphones when not at home.

Choosing the Right Device

You must tailor the choice of device to you, the person who will be using it. Think about your ability, for example, if you can use a remote control for a television you may be able to use a device such as tablet, MP3 player etc. Consider size, shape and functionality of a device as well as when and where you may wish to use it. For example, will it be portable if you are away from home, on holiday or visiting family.

Headphones

Equipment such as headphones can create a personalised listening experience if you enjoy using them. Headphones can help to fix your attention on your own playlist when you are in a public room surrounded by other people and competing sounds – or simply if you have difficulty in concentrating.

About the Author

John has spent over 35 years as a provider of health and social care in both the public and private sectors, This includes running his own domiciliary care business. John also cared for his own father who had dementia. As a talented musician he combined his experience of caring and music to create 'Soundtrack to My Life', a music book for people with dementia. In 2012 it won a national care award for innovation.

John, together with his wife Hazel, founded the charity 'musicworks' to support music and musicians in 1995. They support 'Music in Care' projects such as 'Soundtrack to My Life' through a variety of fundraising activities.

In 2012 he established JoCo Learning & Development to develop and deliver 'Soundtrack' training for health and social care staff. John is a passionate believer that high quality care is a right and not a privilege.

If you have been inspired by the content and approach of this book you may also be interested in the other publications in the ***'Music in Care'*** *series.*

- ***'Soundtrack to My Life'*** *for people with memory loss conditions including dementia.*
- ***'My Music Oasis'*** *for carers either professionally or caring for family members.*
- ***'My Story in Music'*** *for people with life-limiting conditions or at end of life.*
- ***'Music is Medicine'*** *for people undergoing long term medical treatment.*
- ***'My Journey in Music'*** *for young people and those with Asperger's Syndrome and Autism (with Luke Fiddes)*

If you wish to further your knowledge and understanding of 'Music in Care' practice, educational programmes are available from JoCo Learning & Development.

About JoCo Learning & Development Ltd.

JoCo provides a range of health & social care training and consultancy services.

Recognising that musical practice skills of frontline staff are generally ignored, they have developed 'Soundtrack to My Life' training. This is a fun and interactive course for healthcare and social care professionals, activity coordinators and musicians to explore the power and use of personalised music in dementia care. 'Soundtrack to My Life' is a programme for every one, whether you have musical skills or none at all.

For more information about 'Soundtrack to My Life', 'Music in Care' or other health and social care training, visit their website.

www.joco.gb.net

About **musicworks**

Music is central to our experience of the world around us. It is a primary source of the way we experience, understand and interpret the world in which we live. It is one of the core experiences that define us, unite us and enrich us.

musicworks *exists to promote all forms of music by encouraging, recognising and showcasing musicians work to help them reach a wider audience.*

As believers in the power of music we are proud to support ***'Music in Care'****.*

www.musicworksnet.co.uk

* 9 7 8 1 7 8 4 5 6 4 1 5 5 *

ND - #0197 - 060826 - C0 - 210/148/5 - PB - 9781784564155 - Gloss Lamination